I Wish My Words Were Colors

A Collection of Finished and Incomplete Poems and Short Stories from the Past Ten Years

CHARLES JOSEPH

Copyright © 2014 Charles Joseph

All rights reserved.

ISBN: 0991656903
ISBN-13: 978-0-9916569-0-5

DEDICATION

I go to page one,

I have not yet begun.

Nothing's there yet,

But soon will be something

I'll never forget.

Dedicated to the boy who wrote the poem above, the people who never stopped believing in him, and the girl who doesn't know she is his muse.

CONTENTS

	A Letter from the Author	i
1	Penning Poems	1
2	Implementing Idioms	70
3	Teaching Terms	78
4	Making Micro-Fiction	91
5	Conclusion	98

A LETTER FROM THE AUTHOR:

Thank you.

- CJ

P.S. The poems in this collection read by section in (roughly) chronological order. The first poem you read was the first poem I wrote. Penning Poems has more early work than recent pieces as I started Implementing Idioms and Teaching Terms (to myself) in the last two years of the period and focused most-ish of my time on same.

P.P.S. When you read recent pieces did you think about my favorite candy?

PENNING POEMS

The Beast

The beast is unchained
trapped in a bullpen
it paces relentlessly.

After hours it has mellowed
inspected by men,
pictures taken silently.

Then orange branded
hoof prints taken,
prodded quickly.

Into cages forced
with beastly brethren,
it survives hardly.

Away

Today I awoke with nothing to do
so I decided to think of you
Today I stood and counted my blessings
to you my darling my love I'm confessing
Today I sat with the world on my shoulders
I know without you that world would be colder
Today I walked with a spring in my stride
thinking of you, I was grinning quite wide
Today I laid with my hear all a-flutter
you again in my head, my mind in the gutter
Today I slept dreaming baby
my love for you nearly driving me crazy

Coffee with Cream

Skin, colored like that of the sweetest creamed coffee.

Beautiful delicious brown, blazing hot, burnt by a simple touch.

Lovely, luscious, lavish lumps of round mounds that hound to be found, undressed and caressed.

Silky smooth soft strands of sexy hair wisp like smoke in the air when stroked.

I choke on the next words to be spoke.

There's something about you,

crazy, sexy, cool,

that causes me to drool.

Cause it's you.

The one from my dreams with skin colored like coffee with cream.

I WISH MY WORDS WERE COLORS

Same Title as the Popular Songs by Tupac and David Bowie

I did the crime, now I'm doing the time
behind bars at the age of eighteen, wonder why I'm mean.

Nothing you can say can phase me, I'm twisted in the head-
halfway to crazy, pray someday that the devil will blaze me.

I know I'm going to hell, 'cause like Satan I fell from heaven.
Evil since the age of seven, and nothing's changed in the last eleven.

Years, except now I'm here, realized my fears
Cried too many tears and been shunned by my peers.

So it's time for a change, back to normal from strange
A chance to rearrange the emotion from pain

to good. To Good.

An Ugly Color

Orange.
Everywhere
Scared?
Ha! Barely
Were thee
in the place of me
maybe
you'd be,
but me?
Nah.
Been there before,
kind of a bore.
I know what's in store,
but at my core
my heart is tore.
Why?
I no longer want to die
tears fall from no eye
I speak no lie
know why?
Ready for life
sick of strife
a wife?
Not yet,
but bet
when I meet her
and greet her
I won't be in orange.

Time Passes

As feelings become thoughts,
time passes.
As thoughts become words,
time passes.
As words move from brain through arm to hand to finger to pencil
to paper,
time passes.
As words become phrases, sentences, paragraphs, pages,
time passes.
As the pencil dissipates in my hand and becomes dwarfed in relation,
time passes.
So I continue writing despite
                blisters forming on fingers,
            hand cramps,
          calluses,
        why?
                                    Because time passes.

Fragmentary Poems for a Fragmentary Relationship

Like a rope around my heart
You have a hold of me
And ever since the start
I knew how it would be

No matter what you asked for
Big, small, or in-between
I'd want to give you that and more
Because you are my queen

Since the time of our first kiss
You've been on my mind
You're all and more that I could wish
And I love it that you're mine

Someday we may be married
And have babies of our own
If you left me it'd be scary
I'd be stranded all alone

But I know we'll stay together
Because our love is strong
It may not be forever
But it should be very long

You and your rope
You have no control

I won't bow down

Forget the first exchange of fluids
A trap.

Strong?
Forever?

Wrong.

.

Negative Inversion #2- Good Times

The thoughts cannot be stopped
Memories, they do not fade
When I start to miss you
I think of better days

When we would sit together
With nothing else to do
Times when we would watch TV
And I'd hold on to you

Countless days and countless nights
Spent lying on a couch
Kissing, hugging, loving
Living in your mouth

Our birthdays in September
Dinners at those places
When I close my eyes I imagine all your faces

The cute one when you start to laugh
The beautiful one when you smile
The face you make when you say my name
The one that drove me wild

If I had a day to live
That would be alright
If I spent that day with you
I'd be happy with my life

I'm not the greatest person
To ever walk the earth
But I've given you my heart
For all that it is worth

I hope you feel the way for me

I WISH MY WORDS WERE COLORS

The way I feel for you
I hope that you love me back
And I am not a fool

This is by far the hardest thing
I've ever had to do
To sit here and do nothing
And pray that you will too

I'm sorry that this happened
And that I had to leave
It hurts so much sometimes
I tear up as I grieve

But this is when I think
Of those better times
Looking to the future
As we live on our lives

They say you never know
What the future holds
But I know this darling
You're my rainbow's pot-of-gold.

Negative Inversion #2- Bad Times

Thoughts stop
Memories fade
I never miss you
There are no better days

We don't sit
I have things to do
I never watch TV
And never touch you

Day, Night
It's a dirty old couch
Forget you
And the disease in your moth

I don't go out
No dinners, no places
I don't have eyes
There are no faces

No laughs
No smiles
No one says my name
No one drives me wild

I am dying, but
It's alright
If I never saw you
I'd be happy with my life

Amazing alien
I don't walk this earth
Tin man with no heart
It had no worth

I WISH MY WORDS WERE COLORS

You don't feel for me
I don't feel for you
Never love me back fool
This easy thing I can do
Standing, acting? me too

I'm happy this happened
I wanted to leave
It doesn't hurt
I didn't grieve

No thoughts
Of better times
We have no future
We have no lives

I know
What the past holds
Fuck you darling
You are fool's gold

Pre-fight Interview

My words
are going to be
so absurd
that I want you to rewind this tape
play it back
and memorize it
to explain your fate.
Stop, wait,
before you start to hate
give me the chance, to elaborate.
Please, let me demonstrate
how great
I rate
and how you relate.
I'm never late.
I procreate
at a reasonable height
and weight.
See I stimulate
and infatuate.
Copulate
and populate.
While you and your mate
can't corroborate
on your state,
thus you dissipate
can't extrapolate
and don't substantiate
or validate.

While I authenticate
so get it straight.
You're indigent
and ignorant
while I'm diligent.
So that's why I'm confident
I'm the best on this, and every continent.
See you need to remember
you're going to surrender
'cause you're a pretender
and I'm the contender.

Cocaine

It's insane
going from nose
past eye
to membrane.
Do you hear?
This may cause a tear.
Although a gummer
can make you number
it's a bummer
'cause a few rails
might land you in jail

Wausau

Nothing's wrong
and nothings right
All alone
is how I spend my nights
I stay up
smoking on my pipe
it's all I can do
to feel alright

I got friends
but never call them
'cause in the end
I know my brain stem
is the safer
for it
and I cannot
ignore this

Got a job
that barely pays
all alone
is how I spend my days
trying to
get dazed
it's the only way
to forget the pain

The Lovers on the Bus

I truly believe I am in the presence of, and witnessing love,
in its purest and most amazing form.
Love unhindered by looks or even sight.
Pure happiness, unaffected by media's perception.
Two lovers.
Both, dare I say it –
horribly ugly, disabled, retarded.
But yet,
The love and happiness radiates off of them like warm rays of
sunshine piercing even the most impenetrable force.
And just like that they're gone.
They get off the bus holding hands together in a way I cannot
fathom, comprehend, or ever hope to share with anyone.
I am grateful to have shared an ever brief moment with the modern
day Romeo and Juliet.

CHARLES JOSEPH

Figuring it Out

Thoughts. Feelings. Words.
Construed on a page, roughly.
Hope. Observing. Waiting.
Laying, sitting, one side, the other.
Reading. Writing.
Pain, hope. Hope.
Knowing.

Knowing.
I know.
Know what?
The right thing to do.
Easy? No.
Hard? Maybe.
Change, commitment, effort.
Hard? Yea.
Worth it? Yea.
Know what to do? Yes!
You know?
Know what?
The right thing to do.
I know.
Knowing.

I WISH MY WORDS WERE COLORS

Rock Springs

And this town I pass through daily
it is dying
pot holes covered by sand
as opposed to fixed with concrete
speaks to the fleeting quality of life
as concrete would cost more
and its permanence perhaps unnecessary.

The Wolves

They   Know
like Cerberus forever together
bonded by imminent extinction
eyes shooting questions shooting eyes
asking why in such despair
that fie-ry, burning stare
a dignified air
is it true their
whole
gener
ation
dies?

The Odyssey

In clip I, a twirling lay
A detainee from Guantanamo bay
The journey it is fine-ly done
Father, I would like some rum

Pariah of society I ran
Round and round but locked in land
Thought I might just disappear
Swam right round and wound back here

Tried my best, but no way out
Tired from running all about
Became hungry, even famished
So I went hunting, took my chances

Couldn't quite catch the rabbit
Saw a crab and tried to stab it.
Missed, so pissed I sat right down
On the beach with a frown
But then I met to me a dear
Took me in, gave me beer
Became a good friend to me
As I recovered energy

I WISH MY WORDS WERE COLORS

When I was better, full of vigor

Told my out, so I figure

A silt shoal he detailed

Thank you much Mister Snail

So I sit, with you now

Free at last and told you how

Persecution easily avoided

But no! What's that? I've been reported?

Bring Odysseus over there

Strip him down, make him bear

The Scottish Maiden doesn't wait

This time he can't escape his fate

Cui Placet Obliviscitur, Cui Olet Meminit

Fall down drunk we arrived
stumbled up steps and
clumsily stripped
leaving a breadcrumb trail of clothes back to the front door.

The next thing I remember
is how her breath reeked in the morning of cigarettes and whiskey
but I didn't care as we embraced each other
and she told me how she missed me.

I lay there for hour playing doctor
exploring the curves of her body
as if six months would make her
not her.

We had performed this dance before
pretending our past wasn't real.
Cicero was wrong:
We forget our sufferings,
we remember our pleasures.

Lovely Sky Today

It's a lovely sky today.

life seems dull
like steel drums
looks so dreary

listen struggling devil
live some day
love, sing, dream

let sexy demon
ladies strip down
lust, steal, desire

look sap do
little spectacular delicacy
leave, skip, dance

life seems dreamy
like splendid daylight
looks so delightful

It's a lovely sky today.

It's a lovely sky today.

CHARLES JOSEPH

Expanding Consciousness on a Snowy Monday Evening

Can you feel my brain?
It bu   rst like a fire work
s

p r a

y i n g

thoughts

a   c   r   o   s   s

the sky

I was just standing here and my being imploded
loose moral fibers held my conscience like a sieve
as my soul became slicing shrapnel
essence exploded from the hole in the center of my stomach
power personality pushed
effervescent energy erupted
and thoughts tore through
A great white light engulfed an entire nation
visibility was rendered null via excessive exciting experimentation
Do you not
remember me
Do you not
remember that day

Do you want me to take you there?

I WISH MY WORDS WERE COLORS

Did you say   what you said

      or did I hear   what I heard

           do you know   what I'm saying

                         five

             minutes

   ago

                         five

                         minutes

                         from

                         now

                         Or

                   has

              it

         been

      five

years

Let us

    ride

        this ridiculous

                radical   rollercoaster

                        rainbow   all

                                            the

I WISH MY WORDS WERE COLORS

                        wrinkles. Frolic

               rippling   through

        round   freckle

     Run   fields

there.   Plod

way   past

                    palm

                        plains

              Swim

          across

         saliva

       swamps

    Osmotically

move

     armored

        epidermis.

Take the trip right into your cornea

Travel my way into your brain

Am I not   Jesus

Am I not   Albert Einstein

Am I not   Bob Marley

Am I not   My Father

Do I only exist   when my parables are recited

                            when my preachings are taught

                            when my practices are followed?

Am I not   You

Can I not become You at any time

I can voyage inside of You - You cannot impede me

I am all powerful

I create life

I take it

I am

GOD

I WISH MY WORDS WERE COLORS

At any time close my eyes

Shut　　down　　　the system

Crawl inside my own mind

the deepest darkest grotto of thought

where the daylight dies

And you don't exist

but if I so decide

I can o　　pen my eyes

Re　　boot

recreate your life

we exist again

in the little period

at the end of this sentence

in my mind ●

Animal Man

There is no tomorrow
because there is no today
the earth never sleeps
so I won't give away
any chance to be happy
to laugh, sing, and play
because time isn't real
it could go any day.

And when the end comes
Earth's ashes will float
in a sea of stellar darkness
let's hope there's a boat
that finds this transmission

these musical notes

so they'll know we were here

and to them we'll boast

We were put on this planet

third rock from the sun

none of us planned it

but we think we've won

top of the food chain

number one in command

mighty my reign

I'm the animal man.

Bachelor's Anthem

It seems so ridiculous to me
when there's so many fish in the sea
to be stuck with one
and then you're done
for the rest of eternity.
Maybe because
I have more love
that I can share equally?

Baraboo

I have an apartment now, lucky me

a regular member of society.

Got a fake fire place I can't even use

when all I really need is a place for some booze.

In the fake fireplace is fake wood that can't burn

no matter how long flames dance, this wood it stands firm

but leave there no doubt

if word goes by mouth

it's not eternal, but just waiting its turn.

Nothing

That sick summer gray

won't let me get away

from the thoughts in my head

someday we'll be dead

A minor technicality

causes one major tragedy

our lives a travesty

because of the brutality

of nothing.

Nothing between us

can you tell me why

I let my life pass me by

feelings kept locked up inside

stopping daily to ask why

we don't see

what could be

right in front of you and me

I WISH MY WORDS WERE COLORS

Will there be the capacity

to contain curiosity

strong responsibility

or a lack of maturity

or nothing.

You know we all pay

for the things we don't say

as time slips away

and our lives fade to gray

I can't become a casualty

to this nonsense formality

let's forget infinity

and focus on being free

of nothing.

Contemplation

You ask me why I have so much free time

I could answer, I could explain why

but I don't know if you would understand my mind

because I have been to the other side

when you get there you will know

it's the place where nothing grows

nothing living, nothing dead.

Just you inside of your own head.

Fill in the Blank

I've seen the promised land, I've been there once before

it all began, when the fans came through the door

they started grooving, all were getting down

and there weren't any ___ in the crowd

I thought I was dreaming, this couldn't be real

my vision hazy, lost the sense to feel

moving as one, flowing in unison

the stage disappears, and now I am here

Everyone weightless, flying around

I swear not a soul's feet were on the ground

and on this evening, all were content

'cause everyone's twisted, but no one's bent

Time

On the battlefields in my brain
A dead soldier becomes a stain
With no remorse soaks acid rain
On the battlefields in my brain

Last Wishes

Burn my ashes so there's no place to mourn
let my memory live in their hearts like the day I was born
let the wind blow me across this world
the breeze comes you know
I'm the chill in your bones.

CHARLES JOSEPH

Ramblin'

Trying to save her
cause I owed her a favor,
she thought it'd be amusing
to start the storm a brewing.
I need a savior,
something to phase her.
Came up with an illusion,
cause my life was in ruin.

I don't know why
I say die
when you come around.
Leaving this town
is what I'm doing.
Cause I've been pursuing
a brand new flavor,
one I can savor.

Ships on the Sea

Seemingly smart sailors sail silently south as seagulls scream scratchily

The Lovers On the Bus Revisited

My mind has deleted the images off the hard drive,
I don't remember what they look like anymore.

But it doesn't matter,
because I was there.

No picture could serve purpose to what I experienced.
No painting could suffice.
And certainly no poems,
no matter how nice,
could do justice to

That day.
Five glorious minutes when I received the ultimate gift,
witnessing true love.
While I may not remember faces and details,
I remember

That feeling.
Euphoria and ecstasy
better than any pill, snort, or smoke.

And also the insane jealously,
that my life in comparison was a joke

But I am not bitter, nay,
I'm thankful I was there
That day.

The Search

I'm not an actor playing off cues

experience factor is just old news

you don't know me, you don't know my blues

A simple poet searching for my muse.

If someday I find the woman I would choose

caution to the wind, I'll break all rules

calling three days later is really for fools

time is of the essence if you're the fuel for my fuse.

Marketing

Delicious, nutritious, and only slightly sacrilegious

Love in Winter

a roman soldier

my helmet is the boulder

as we get older

The Far Side

Do it – the duet.

There's got to be a place to call.

It's the logical conclusion.

A body language expert

or spider.

Four people.

One is good,

one lives in a phone booth,

one lives in the basement,

one lives in a cupboard.

Playing a game.

On large concrete staircase

with a hole in it.

CHARLES JOSEPH

Ochpaniztli

Crazy water clear

Pay your daughter do not fear

Day of slaughter here

Depression in Middle Class America?

The thoughts in your head
Put there with no care
By people near dead
With gray wispy hair

But everything's fine
You eat all the time
Never fear famine,
disease, death, or crime.

War of the Sons of Light against the Sons of Darkness

Sit and stare a fiery glare.

Determination on their brow.

Hark as the herald angel screamed.

Question Asked at the Crossroads

can the devil be

a friend to me?

Obliquity

> Two people can be
> in love with each other at
> different times, sigh.

Beautiful Medusa

when I look into your eyes I turn to stone.

one moment, a thousand life times lived together in the most amazing instant ever experienced.

pure happiness.

From Beneath the Hard Earth

the
hands
of
the
dead
cannot
steady
the
work
of
the
living
luckily
the
cold
rain
quenches
their
thirst

Paranoia

We all keep drinking the water.
It makes us crazy

best poetry comes from us tortured

Do not fret, do not fight. Everything will be alright.

Pastor of the Brave

master of your slave
on the ashes of your grave
enslaved by the slaved

I WISH MY WORDS WERE COLORS

Black Market

name your vice

Fly Away with me in Revelry

a woman lover
perceived as a womanizer
watch me surprise her

Bane of the Brain

I think the bane of existence is
having a brain and
being able to remember.

Replaying last night's missteps
over and over.

I should have said this,
I should have done that and
it all becomes so crystal clear.

Thus, it's fitting I
spend so much time
throwing punches at a mirror,

when the only person
I am battling
is myself.

Tossing jabs at fight-less air

as if I were

without a care.

I WISH MY WORDS WERE COLORS

I wish I could

channel my rage

into useful fury.

But, I'm losing it.

My hair,

my mind,

my life.

This is how people become jaded.

Faded, bladed, debated.

Twist

Peter walked.
He enjoyed walking.
Liked it much better than talking.
So, Peter walked.
Occasionally,
someone would stop Peter to talk,
but Peter pressed on.
Eventually,
Peter grew tired of walking.
And
wanted to do some talking .
but when he stopped his walk
There was no one left
with which to talk.
Poor Peter.

Irony & Suspense

Ecstasy

has caused me

great pain.

Sensations

waking up
it's you again
am I a slut
are you my friend

we never talk
anymore
just fuck on cot,
couch, or floor

do you feel
like a whore
is this real
or a chore

first to leave
does the favor
but final heave
they're the savior

The Most Beautiful Girl in the World

If I had a dollar
For every time I just sat and stared.
I mean I see your face in pictures as I scroll
Then I think I should say something
So I click on your profile
To open it up
And I leave it
For later
As a reminder to say something
And it sits.
Open on my screen for hours, days.
Until I scold myself for thinking I would say something
And close the page.
Until it happens again.
You post a picture doing things I wish I was
And I stare at your eyes. [1]
Wondering what to say, how to start, and if it's even worth it.
I mean.
You.
And.
I.
We don't even talk.
So how receptive could you be to a confession of ~~love~~ ~~lust~~ desire?
And it wouldn't be easy because
Your beautiful and positive and probably have lots of guys who want you but I'm
Just
A
Friend's
Friend.
And one who you don't really talk to.
But I know we had something, once.

I WISH MY WORDS WERE COLORS

A back and forth
With you in that black dress
That ended exactly as I'd hoped.
But its nearly six years later
And
We live nearly six hours apart by car
So
What's.
The.
Use.
Am I supposed to write you a long letter
Telling you exactly this?
That if we lived in the same city,
I would have asked you a million times by now[2] to be with me
Or for dinner, or drinks, or something.
But we don't.
So I haven't.
But it has finally driven me so mad I feel the need to crash it into you
And confess everything.
That I would travel the distance to you for the chance to see if it was worth a move
Because
Who knows.
Maybe.

---

[1] I could say something here about your eyes being the same clear blue as the freshest waters and I want to bathe and baptize myself in them but let's be honest your eyes aren't cool blue pools waiting to be dove into, but rather a deep abyss in which to get lost.

[2] Even then I probably wouldn't know how.

Today

Looking at pictures of people you've never met
Pretending something's wrong and you're upset.

So lonely you wish
You would get catfished.

Banging away on the keyboard you type
Fighting and striving to save your life.

It isn't jealously, it isn't rage
It's the modern digital age.

Flight

Float. Flutter. Fly.
My thoughts race across the sky.
Time to think. Time to drink. Time to draft a note for pink.
The pressurized cabin leads to great release and peace.
Weight off the chest lifted by text.
Thoughts In head finally make their way to page, to note.
Written once and never spoke.
Float, Flutter, fly. My thoughts race across the sky.

CHARLES JOSEPH

Summer Runner

Sometimes it is fun

to get out and run, till you

are tired and done

Seattle

It's magnificent

where mountain and cloud mix

melting into the horizon

becoming ocean.

Vernal Equinox

The sunset's song suffers from the drone of darkness

The snow relaxes as its tormentor drifts away

A few more hours of night

Is what it needs today

Modified Epiphanies of a Prophet (Revelations Occurring on Trips)

And if thoughts flowed like dominos,
I'd be living in the Poconos,
but this writer's block -
you know.

One thousand critics
stabbing my ear with their pens.
I want to break,
'cause I'm done with the bends.

But the only satisfaction I find
is consuming my mind.

The explosion when everything makes sense.
Because life is as wonderful and complex
as this thought the one minute
and that the next.

So what is death,
other than being remembered?

The ultimate paradox once lost,
those left behind
have less on their minds.

Since he who writes that into being is - I endure.
Proving the pen is always mightier
the end changes with its writer.

Dyestuff, Tincture, Banderole, Blush

I wish my words were colors.
I'd paint you a pretty picture
and you'd frame it and hang it in your house.
But my words aren't colors.
They're just words.
Black and white and bland on a page.

So I rhyme
and use time
to move them around.
Like a clown
trying my best
to turn your frown
upside-down.

If my words were colors
they'd be the most fun ones
like jazzberry jam and razzmatazz,
fuzzy wuzzy brown and purple pizzazz.
But my words aren't colors.
They're just words.
Black and white and bland on a page.

Thus this won't get framed or hanged with your things,
but will sit on a shelf or collect coffee rings,
if not some data on a device that's digital –
deleted one day for something less difficult.
So rather than words colored neon carrot and laser lemon,
I'm using ones I won't thrice mention.

You won't gaze at them all the time,
read once then tossed aside.
Feelings conveyed , quickly forgotten –
for only a second sentiment begotten.
So maybe my words are better than colors,
understood for a moment and spread to others.

cricket

the night, the night

i sing for the night.

Apologetic Love

And I think back and the fact that this is the first poem I wrote for her and I think that says all it needs. Because mine weren't met.

But that statement is not completely true or false. And although ours was less than a perfect love, that was mostly my fault. So, sorry.

Peter's Point of View

They say the journey of a thousand miles

starts with a step,

mine's been a serpentine stroll

and its brought me here –

with half my verses written for a woman

who doesn't exist

that I've never met

who I'll never kiss.

Of course,

I can always close my eyes

and the phosphenes become

beautiful naked neon women

spinning on a fluorescent merry-go-round.

But,

like a bug it doesn't matter –

the winner loses,

and the loser wins,

the swinger sings the blues,

and the blues begin.

A Nugatory Nugget

The secret
to being prolific
is putting it
down on paper

Displeased Patrons

I rue the roux! Said the cook
who's name got taken off the books
for serving his new recipe
without this soup necessity.

Title

What if I tried to write a poem that didn't rhyme
or use words I don't know
or sayings I don't use
or tricks
or mimic
or steal.

Something totally and completely original.
It would probably be bad.
No pattern.
Or syllable count
No deep descriptions.
and definitely no similes.
Just some stupid fucking words slapped together

Because who cares.
Is some epic poem going to change the world?
It probably won't even change your mind.

So I talk to myself
why are you even doing this?
    -   my legacy.
you don't have one
    -   exactly.

Spring Mix

no bumper sticker

ever changed my life but one

it said eat more kale

Modified Epiphanies of a Prophet (Revelations Occurring on Trips) - Concluded

P.S. And the meaning of life? It's love.

And I want to feel love again.

ed
IMPLEMENTING IDIOMS

Success

Shooting fish in a barrel

Is game not worth the candle

It turns you all hat and no cattle.

Throw sprat to catch mackerel

When up creek without paddle

Sometimes it's half the battle.

Wisconsin

I am cheesed off with all this cheese-paring

Aren't you supposed to be a big cheese?

Well hard cheese if you don't like it,

But someone cut the cheese during the last picture

So say cheese 'cause we are doing another!

I WISH MY WORDS WERE COLORS

Is it Me You're Looking For?

I cut my eyes at her, but didn't talk and could only smile.

Words would be a dog's breakfast, not first sight or puppy style.

But the course of it true never did run smooth.

And you can't have your cake and eat it too.

'Cause it's catch as catch can.

Whether woman or man.

And I hope it's as blind as believed because

With a face only a mother does

I don't know if I could get her for it or money

But the best way to catch flies is with honey

So if all is fair, I'll help it find a way

By getting on my horse today.

Hello.

Epiphany pre-Slumber

Here I am fiddling while Rome burns.
Marching to the beat of my own drum and
tooting my own horn about
being fit as a fiddle and
all that jazz.

When it's clear as a bell
I need some fine tuning if
I want to call the tune because
the thing about bells is
 you can't unring them.

I should hit the right note
maybe play second fiddle and
whistle Dixie to strike a chord.

To be there with bells on
costs only a song
and while there are some
who want me to whistle for it –

I WISH MY WORDS WERE COLORS

it takes two to tango.

So I'll change my tune

before I face the music

After all,

this is a whistle-stop tour and

it's time to pull out all the sojourns for

my swan song so

I can hear

music to my ears.

See you on the big drum.

CHARLES JOSEPH

The Way to Make a Large Number of Hearts and Minds Follow is?

with a vice grip on the testes of life.

Bottoms-up

The well-oiled fly flew in

decorating the mahogany

with champagne taste on a beer budget.

His head no better than one on a nickel

drowning his sorrows

over small beer he whined.

After wetting his whistle

he fluttered to the next stop

three sheets to the wind.

I WISH MY WORDS WERE COLORS

Don't Know Whether to Wind a Watch or Bark at the Moon

since my loose moral fiber holds my conscience like a sieve

both lover, fighter hold their conference with a shiv

one wants to be a champagne socialist in a May-December romance alive as amaranth

the other a Champlain novelist , go away and reenter perchance like a coelacanth

maybe one is chasing rainbows and will never end up on cloud nine

the other placing reign low, an ill endeavor corrupt, un-proud, benign

perhaps the stone with no moss will roll into tall cotton

lapse atoned, paid cost of toll, to all forgotten

or the belated bloomer will prosper, day in the sun, better late than never

culminated with a schooner in Gloucester, brays and stunts sequestered no wait for measure.

TEACHING TERMS

The Subject Reads the Predicate

With my eyes are so close to her.

The little blonde hairs make her legs seem fimbriated.

With futility I'm exasperated,

My feelings becoming exacerbated.

I, a cat's-paw

Willingly participating in the foofaraw

Was crossing the Rubicon

Betwixt here and gone

Another hapless captive in her coffle

A punctilious minion for her brothel

Like an obsequious neonate I lay silent as she leafed through my lucubration

And I don't know how she, a polyglot, could not translate my tergiversation.

Although perhaps she could surmise my vocation

Was an attempt to devise persuasion

But chose not to chastise my narration

With a Dash of Don Juan

In the nidus of my brain

I metic-lously arrange

Odious lust

To incorporeal dust

Limiting the rabble's decry.

Yet, I concede I remain pertinacious

My pastiche will enervate the tenacious

By firing poetic fusillade

Followed with expressive escalade

I'll win desire and accolade.

Making me, a picaro

A modern day Cicero.

I WISH MY WORDS WERE COLORS

Stockholm

Traveling to our destination, I unraveled this – his explanation.
Gavel struck with contemplation, gravel sleep the condemnation.
Bounty said to be a foison, needed alive so they could poison
As we journeyed and I persuaded, he became the right kind of jaded.

One day, seemingly swift, the mercurial trepan released me as a gift
Here at the zenith of a fecund couloir, having gained motility pulled skill from repertoire.

Prestidigitation led to my non-pecuniary purchase of his musket, which made our goodbye less valedictory obeisance but far more rustic.

Invocations answered, my abductor had become hoisted by his own petard.
Flouting the law, I left him for a long repose to begin this town's boneyard.

Missed Connection

We met at a hotel bar.
Not a bar in a hotel,
but a bar named after one.

And while we hit things off,
please consider this,
that discussion's corrigendum.

I believe your name was Bailey,
but, to be honest,
memory fails me.

On the patio, I breached your entourage
with confidence and badinage
before wishing you brief bon voyage.

Till seeing you downstairs again,
as you were getting water for a friend,
began speaking as if our first talk didn't end.

I WISH MY WORDS WERE COLORS

You asked me what I want to do

and drunkenly I answered you

and told you I would tell the truth.

But I, no sycophant and thinking little of reprobation,

talked with disproportion and without cessation

about my goals, hopes, and a particular aspiration.

Never once asking you

what you want to do

or if you like, what I like too.

Stultifying drinks having hampered my skills at pre-dating,

no number asked for as I was torpid in consummating

and thus left sodden and on this page narrating.

So if perchance at this you glance

and decide I deserve a second chance,

contact me for love and romance.

Fish out of Water

I can't infer your wonts.

Feeling aberrant I abscond.

Metacognition

A series of eristic quibbles and trumpery.

likely to be enskied by the loquacious

but fricasseed by the sagacious.

Sporadic gormless tomfoolery that forfends me benific work.

Acacious

As I'm perspicacious I noticed your behavior ostentatious

and feeling audacious I became loquacious

while you appeared disputatious my sense sagacious

determined this fallacious and feeling rapacious

spoke to you flirtatious hoping it to be efficacious

I was vivacious as I described your body curvaceous

and likely seemed salacious, or at best voracious

but you were gracious and gave an excuse mendacious

I WISH MY WORDS WERE COLORS

The Butch Coolidge Question

The pugilist's perseverance had placed him in a predicament

Abeyance was the best bet, but he'd be beset with bewilderment

Abdicating his thrown, supplanted by a style skinflint

The Gigolo Litterateur

There stood Lamont
with his chest bouffant
as was his wont.

Taking floozies
 to the movies,
he was quite the doozy.

Wearing chintz when he sprints
he squints for a hint
or glimpse of the glint

out of this stint
of print and reprint
on lint

'cause he don't make a dint.

Prolepsis - The Critic

An androcentric
and narcissistic
hallucinogenic user like Hendrix.

A hopeless romantic
obsessed with semantics
who expects me to be sycophantic.

If his frantic antics
are authentic
then he's maybe hypomanic
and certainly eccentric.

Rarely iambic
he thinks he's gigantic
clearly egocentric
the sun heliocentric.

But a clever gambit, to be candid –
hope he makes out like a bandit.

Long-term Unrequited Long-distance Love

This was the shoal of my soul, the chasm in my plasm

The status quo ante made me pococurante

But dawn of my discord was not nebulous

Outrance made the springboard turn tenuous

The lacuna in my pneuma

I thought her my Luna

even as I inveighed my mind's duma

to consider her Fortuna

and another tuna in the laguna

Thus, my antics continue like protocol

Skylarking through falderal

Parol careering at any femme fatale

Playing the game a cheval

Ultimately on a journey like Heyerdahl

MAKING MICRO-FICTION

The Talk to Home

An old man and a young man are walking back to their village through the forest. It is night and very dark. They whisper approaching the orange glow of home.

"Young man, you know not what you speak. You talk of peace, but remember the elders and why we fight."

"The elders preach from tattered texts! They are but parrots repeating the words of the dead and we sheep being herded towards demise."

"Young man, you are too green, I think you need some sleep. You spew blasphemous treason. Quiet now as we approach."

"Old man, if peace is but a pipe dream, then it is smoked from the shells of hollowed bombs."

They pause and look at each other.

"Someday, it may be so."

The two men step across the lone and into the circle of structures that creates the village. They walk to the community wash basin and scoop out the cool water with wooden buckets. They wash the blood off their hands in silence.

I WISH MY WORDS WERE COLORS

Down the Rabbit Hole

I hadn't spent six weeks sitting on the cusp of insanity to be shunned. The sweet satisfaction of finding one more piece of this psychopathic puzzle feels at once titillating and fulfilling. He's toying with me. Literally. Leaving this body outside a goddamn Toys 'R Us. I can't wait for His next trick. Maybe He'll try to tell me it's only a game. I should let the sergeant know he needs to start staking out any Milton Bradley factories. I wonder what little gift will be there waiting insider her stomach. Another picture from my past? A piece of clothing? Perhaps my TV remote? The other detectives feel sorry for me. I don't. He wants me to catch Him. Me. If He wanted to kill me, He could. He already would have. He's good and He knows it. Oh, I love the constant randomization of His modus operandi. While most killers have the desire to fill the need with a similar victim, type of kill, or time between kills, my killer is better than that. My killer gets his thrills from toying with *me*, from playing games with us *all*. Rich. Poor, black, white, He discriminates not – I admire Him for that. This is definitely His work, though. The face is removed perfectly, not roughly done by some bullshit copycat killer who can't be creative enough to come up with His *own* signature. I almost hope I never catch this One, I'll never have fun like this again. My own killer, a goddamn real life grim reaper. The torso seems sliced in the normal five-inch incision below the last rib on the right side, perfect to fit a hand into. I know they're all waiting for me to reach in and find what's there for me. This suspense is intoxicating, all these fucking hot-shot cops waiting for me to stick my hand in this poor corpse's gut and grab god knows what. They're disgusted; I see it on their faces. Squirm piggies, squirm. I hope I'm not smiling while I dig for this. All I need is the press getting a picture of me elbows deep with a huge shit-eating grin on my face. What do we have here? Small, square, somewhat sharp edges…interesting. What has my killer left me? He is so smart, so psychotic, I can only imagine. His skill at this game rivals some of the greatest to ever play. I bet the gift isn't a clue at all, but a red herring that will lead us all on a wild goose hunt. Almost got it. A metal square? What is this? My killer has tricked me again: just a square. Maybe I'll clean it off, then there might be a clue – a note or picture or something. A mirror? Ha! Oh, my killer is smart, just another joke, another piece in an endless puzzle. A mirror. Huh, look at that, something in my teeth. Probably from the marinated chicken salad I had at lunch, better get it before the press conference. He has done it again, I am stumped and fooled. A mirror! No one will ever catch this – maybe it's time for a haircut. Some strands are growing over my ears. Interesting. A mirror. What, I suppose He wants me to "look inside myself" in some Zen introspection to catch Him now? He is amazing, too good. Too good! A mirror, of all things, a mirror! He is completely indescribable, too good at what He does, My killer is so good, my killer is, wait a mirror? My killer is…

The Gorge

Then it hit me. I've been here before. I've been here a thousand times and I'll be here a million more. I've lived a thousand lives to get to this point and will live a million more to get to the same. Each time it's exactly the same. Suddenly I realize I'm back and there is nothing I can do to stop it but the next series of events will unfold the way they always have and always will.

Fear, nervousness, and excitement overwhelm me. The concert continues and I know the song before the first note is played. Dancing, she is suddenly in front of me. We have aligned like two planets on an astronomically infrequent celestial path.

Am I orchestrating the next events in my mind and causing them to occur? Or simply predicting them because I've dreamed this? Lived this? Regardless, a magnetism we can't resist moves her closer as if she is floating on waves until she is so close we are nearly touching. My heart stops as I go into shock from the anticipation, then explodes coursing the overwhelming sublime throughout my body. She is so close her hair graces my face as she sways. It is soft and smells just as I remembered. We dance and the fear sets in.

I can't stop this if I tried. I know that this doesn't end well for me because it never does, but I don't care. People move past us, it feels crowded – claustrophobic. She is pushed then pushes back.

Suddenly we touch.

It is magical, glorious, and meant to be. We sway there momentarily and I cautiously hold on to the side of her pant leg as I am overcome with a flood of eternal love.

And just like that it ends. She starts to move away. But more is said in those three second than any words ever could. I am crushed, yet fulfilled. I loved her more in those three seconds than I will ever love anyone again and more than anyone will love her again. Two souls. The only two souls that matter. That truly exist. The prototypes.

We are the reason the world, the universe, exists. For this once in a lifetime alignment when all in the universe is most right and the most pure and the most intense love exists. I'm male and she is female. And we created everyone and everything together, but somehow I screw it up every time and she leaves me.

I am left forever waiting for the perfect moment, the perfect existence when I have the courage to say something. To tell her how intense I feel. That I may have never felt anything so strong before in my life and that I will love her more in those three seconds than anyone else ever could or would.

She moves away towards what seems to be an ex or current lover. They have history, security, and I am a risk and a chance e – no matter how right it feels in the moment.

Launched into despair I curse myself for making the move and touching what ought to be my soul mate. I knew she would return to him. She has before and I'm sure she will again until I can, in some parallel universe, get everything right and win her.

The show continues and I vacillate from thinking I am an idiot and crazy to knowing she felt and knew the truth too, that we are each other's ultimate destiny. I vacillate from thinking I am a God to a Bug. But just when I think I was wrong, She returns and dances near me again, briefly. I grasp her like before, barely, while screaming in my head that I would do anything to be with her, but I cannot speak

– I dare not.

As soon as she is there she is gone. Laughing with her friends likely at me for my foolishness. I care not. Those few glorious moments have justified my existence and I will work towards them again. Maybe someday I'll say something instead of waiting for her to turn and proclaim her love for me.

One of the times I'll get it right and she'll be mine and leave him. One of these times I'll confess my crush, my lust. One of these times I will say exactly what I'm feeling. That I don't know you, but I love you. I have loved you since the first time I saw you and I doubt you know I exist, but yet I dream about you. Not often, but I don't dream often. And this was the most right anything has ever felt in my life.

But the show ends. She returns to him despite my psychedelic thoughts of destiny and love. Did she feel as strongly for me as I did for her? Did she feel anything at all? I don't ask, too afraid to know.

CONCLUSION: THIS PIECE IS FROM ALMOST THE EXACT MIDDLE OF THE PERIOD. I LIKE IT A LOT SO IT'S LAST.

I WISH MY WORDS WERE COLORS

Thirteen Ways of Looking at a Lion
  -   after Wallace Stevens

I.
Among a Roman wilderness of pain
The only feared thing
was the heart of the lion.

II.
Confused
Like a Catholic
Do I confess to the lion?

III.
Lion the soft beast,
Like poppy fields it puts you to sleep.

IV.
Respice Finem.
Lions eat men.
To reveal, to release, to relinquish
Is it to ruin?
Empower repugnant revolting refuse to run rampant?

V.
Did a lion paw lazily at the fresh carcass
When Christ had his moment of doubt and pain?
Will you be lion forever - untamed,
Out of line.
Can I domesticate that cat,
Educate this feline?

VI.

Do I learn by going, even though,
I don't know where I have to go?
I'll ask Roethke, he might know,
He had lions of his own.

VII.

Lion meditating on sins committed,
I realize the worse remorse
Comes from those I didn't.
When I stole, I stole a million,
So the lion is my queen.

VIII.

I'll always say the deal is fair.
I would always trade -
My lifetime as mouse,
To be a lion for a day.

IX.

The lion is no Maltese Falcon.
Pure, it is no trick.
I becoming Ahab,
It, my Moby Dick.

X.

Dunces rise in confederacy,
Swift the sign is here.
Fulfillment of the prophecy,
The genius has appeared.
Wrong place, wrong time slothily,
A lion disappears.

XI.
Vincit Omnia Veritas.
All this drama,
A lion's mask at Mardi Gras.

XII.
As a breeze blows softly through the grass,
The mouse lies screaming.
Darkness digests the Savannah,
The lion must be feasting.

XIII.
I will breathe in deeply,
And say years from now.
That I -
I caught my lion,
And never will say how.

ABOUT THE AUTHOR

I graduated from the University of Wisconsin School of Business and enjoy working for a Fortune 100 company, but prefer poetry over profits and writing over hand-wringing. I travel a lot and do not own a television.

This collection is me. From the trouble in my teen years, to my follies with the fairer sex through college and continuing today.

If you haven't, Press On and Enjoy IT! If you have, Thanks.